Fish Bab

Catherine Veitch

Heinemann
LIBRARY
Chicago, Illinois

© 2013 Heinemann Library
an imprint of Capstone Global Library, LLC
Chicago, Illinois

To contact Capstone Global Library please phone
800-747-4992, or visit our website www.capstonepub.com

Edited by Daniel Nunn, Rebecca Rissman,
and Catherine Veitch
Designed by Cynthia Della-Rovere
Picture research by Ruth Blair
Production by Victoria Fitzgerald
Originated by Capstone Global Library
Printed and bound in China

17 16 15 14 13
10 9 8 7 6 5 4 3 2 1

Library of Congress Cataloging-in-Publication Data
Veitch, Catherine.
  Fish babies / Catherine Veitch.
     pages cm.—(Animal babies)
  Includes bibliographical references and index.
  ISBN 978-1-4329-7493-0 (hb)
  ISBN 978-1-4329-8418-2 (pb)
  1. Fishes—Infancy—Juvenile literature. . I. Title.
  QL639.25.V45 2014
  597.13'92—dc23   2012033023

Acknowledgments
We would like to thank the following for permission to
reproduce photographs: Naturepl pp. title page (© Nature
Production), 6 (© Jane Burton), 7 (© David Fleetham),
8 (© Jurgen Freund), 9 (© Georgette Douwma), 10 (©
Jane Burton), 11 (© Jane Burton), 12 (© Jane Burton), 13
(© David Fleetham), 14 (© Jane Burton), 16 (© Nature
Production), 17 (© Mark Bowler), 19 (© Jane Burton),
20 (© Wild Wonders of Europe / Roggo), 22 (© Jane
Burton, © Angelo Giampiccolo), 23 (© Jurgen Freund);
Shutterstock pp. 4 (© Krzysztof Odziomek), 5 (© Cigdem
Sean Cooper), 15 (© mnoor), 18 (© Dobermaraner), 21
(© Peter Leahy), 22 (© Kletr), 23 (© Kletr, © Cigdem
Sean Cooper).

Front cover photograph of brown discus parent and
babies reproduced with kind permission of Naturepl
(© Nature Production).

We would like to thank Michael Bright for his invaluable
help in the preparation of this book.

Every effort has been made to contact copyright holders
of any material reproduced in this book. Any omissions
will be rectified in subsequent printings if notice is given
to the publisher.

Contents

What Is a Fish?

Fish live in water.

gill

fin

Fish have gills. Fish have fins.

How Are Baby Fish Born?

egg

Most female fish lay eggs.

baby

egg

Sometimes fish babies hatch from eggs.

larva inside an egg

Sometimes larvae hatch from eggs.

Larvae grow into baby fish.

babies inside

Some female fish do not lay eggs.

baby

They give birth to baby fish.

Where Do Fish Lay Their Eggs?

Female fish lay their eggs in the water.

Some fish carry their eggs in their mouths.

nest made from plants

Some fish make nests for their eggs.

bubbles

This nest is made of bubbles.

Caring For Baby Fish

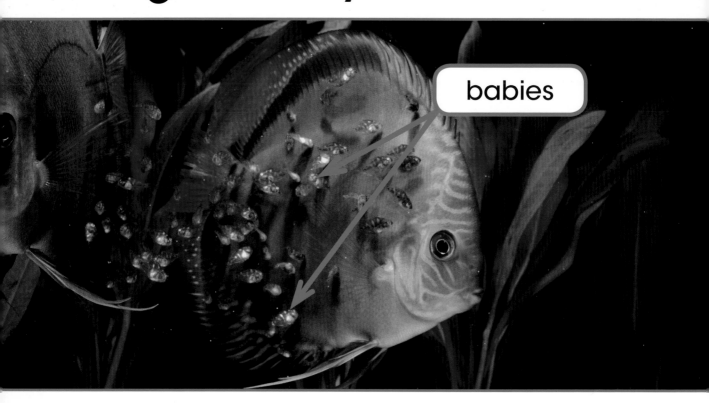

babies

Some fish care for their babies.

baby

This fish carries its babies in its mouth.

Some fish eat their own babies.

The baby fish hide to stay safe.

Growing Up

Most baby fish look after themselves. They feed on insects and plants.

They hide from predators.

Life Cycle of a Fish

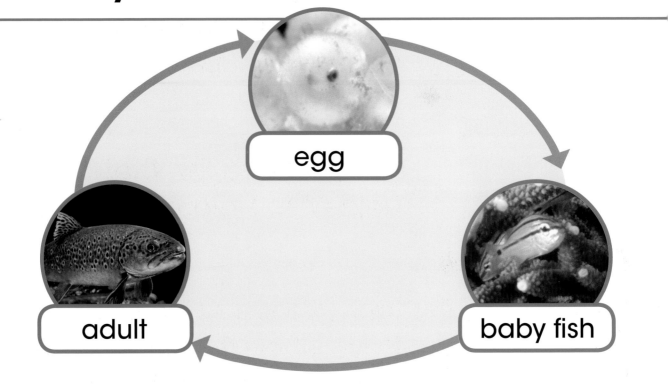

egg

adult

baby fish

A life cycle shows the different stages of an animal's life. This is the life cycle of a fish.

Picture Glossary

 **fin** part of a fish that helps it to swim

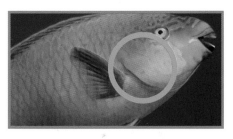 **gill** part of a fish that helps it to breathe

 **larva** stage some fish have when they first hatch. More than one is larvae.

 **predator** animal that eats other animals

Index

Notes to Parents and Teachers

Before reading

Show children a collection of photos and videos of fish. National Geographic and PBS are useful websites. Explain what a fish is and discuss the characteristics of fish.

After reading

- Mount photos of adult and baby fish on note cards and play games of concentration where the children have to match a baby fish with its parent. Model the correct pairs first.
- Ask children to label the parts of a fish: for example, fin, gill, tail, scales.
- Look at page 22 and discuss the life cycle stages of a fish. Mount photos of the egg, baby, and adult stages and ask children to put the photos in order. Encourage children to draw a life cycle of a human to compare. Compare how different fish care for their babies. Discuss the care human babies need.
- To extend children's knowledge, the fish are as follows: perch: p. 4; parrotfish: p. 5; bullhead eggs and fry: p. 6; ray next to an unhatched ray egg: p. 7; clownfish eggs with larvae inside: p. 8; pufferfish: p. 9; swordtail: pp. 10, 11; cichlid: p. 12; jawfish: p. 13; stickleback: p. 14; Siamese fighting fish: p. 15; discus: p. 16; arowana: p. 17; platy: p. 18; trout: p. 19; grayling: p. 20; grunts: p. 21.